Edith Bell

Reminiscences of a Student's Life

Reminiscences
of a Student's Life

Jane Ellen Harrison

Second Impression

Published by Leonard and Virginia Woolf at the
Hogarth Press, 52 Tavistock Square, London, W.C.
1925

First published October 1925.
Reprinted December 1925.

Printed in Great Britain by R. & R. CLARK, LIMITED, Edinburgh.

CONTENTS

CHAPTER I

ILLUSTRATIONS

CHAPTER I

Yorkshire Days

In view of my present cult for Russia and
things Russian, I like to think that my first
childish memory is of the word " Moscow ".
Moscow to me was a dog, not a town—an
old Newfoundland dog named, no doubt, in
honour of the Crimean War, which will
sufficiently date these reminiscences. Moscow
had his kennel in the backyard under a big
spreading tree, and from this tree exuded drops
of bright gum. It was my fearful joy to
rush to the tree, seize the gum-drops which
were well within the length of Moscow's
chain, and be back before he could begin to
bark ferociously. When later I learnt that
to some people Moscow was a cathedral city,
not a dog, my universe rocked with Ein-
steinian relativity. Russia was about us in
those days, a strange, inhuman Russia of Tzars
and Siberia. My first toy was a box of bricks
and soldiers mixed, called " The Siege of
Sevastopol ", given by a patriotic uncle   I

hated soldiers and sieges and muskets and
bayonets, but the word Sevastopol was a
marvel, and a soft joy to my child's mouth. I
turned it over and over, and when much later
I learned its Greek origin and meaning, there
seemed a real fitness in things.

Then, every Christmas came Russia again.
My father had had some business relations
with Russia, and every year some kind Russian
used to send him a package of caviare and
cranberries and reindeers' tongues. The
caviare was reserved for my father, but he
gave me sometimes delicious morsels on hot
toast, and he has left me the legacy of a too
delicate palate. The cranberries were made
into sauce for venison, for the grown-ups'
dinners, but a few reindeers' tongues found
their way to our schoolroom breakfast, where
they were keenly appreciated by one little
greedy fat child. Oh those reindeers' tongues!
they tasted not only of reindeer, but—but of
snow-fields and dreaming forests.

My father had also imported a tiny Russian
sledge, and sometimes he took me for drives—
thank God it only held one, so I could dream
undisturbed of steppes and Siberia and bears
and wolves. All my lore was derived from
two enchanting books—*Near Home* and *Far
Off*. I wish I had them now,[1] but north and

[1] A kind reader of the *Nation* has since supplied my need.

JANE HARRISON (aged five).

To face page 10.

south were jumbled and jostled in my fancies.
Since then I have only once been in a sledge.
When I was spending a winter at S. Moritz
a friend died. Her funeral procession was
a long line of sledges. It was unspeakably
solemn and silent. When I die, if I cannot
be buried at sea, I should like to go to my grave
in a sledge.

But Russia soon faded, leaving only my
native Yorkshire. And here I must make
confession. In politics I am an old Liberal,
with a dash of the Little Englander and the
Bolshevik. I hate the Empire; it stands to
me for all that is tedious and pernicious in
thought; within it are always and necessarily
the seeds of war. I object to nearly all forms
of patriotism. But when I search the hidden
depths of my heart, I find there the most
narrow and local of parochialisms. I am
intensely proud of being a Yorkshire woman.

My gifted friend Hope Mirrlees has
written a wonderful novel, *Counterplot*, in
which she shows that only in and through the
pattern of art, or it may be of religion, which is
a form of art, do we at all seize and understand
the tangle of experience which we call Life.
Until I met Aunt Glegg in the *Mill on the
Floss*, I never knew myself. I *am* Aunt
Glegg; with all reverence I say it. I wear

before the world a mask of bland cosmopolitan courtesy and culture; I am advanced in my views, eager to be in touch with all modern movements, but beneath all that lies Aunt Glegg, rigidly, irrationally conservative, fibrous with prejudice, deep-rooted in her native soil.

It is said by Southerners that we Yorkshire people are exclusive, gruff in manner, harsh and unsympathetic in soul. Gruff in manner I grant it, but our bark is worse than our bite. Exclusive? possibly, yet I have heard a Yorkshire lady say "there are some quite decent people in Scotland." Harsh and unsympathetic in soul. Well. A friend of mine was left by her husband alone in a small moorland cottage they had taken for the summer. At nightfall a knock was heard; her landlord entered, under his arm a large grey rabbit. " I heerd t' Maister had left yer alawn, maybe ye'd be lawnly. I brought t' rabbit; he'd be a bit o' company for yer." I myself was left by a friend in a small Yorkshire inn. The landlady looked in on me in the morning, bearing a huge dead duck. " Yer'll maybe be lawnly wi'out Missie, happen yer'd fancy a dook fer yer dinner." I did, and I ate two huge slices of its fat breast with unlimited savoury trimmings. She looked in to mark my progress. " Aye, yer eat but poorly, yer've been living maybe wi' them Southerners." When I left my inn, I thanked the landlady for all her kindness. She looked at me steadily and said, "It weren't you, I knawed yer fayther, t'aud Charlie 'Arrison." Now my father was never called "Charlie"; he was far too remote and solemn a man for diminutives. She was using what grammarians call—or would call if they ever attended to anything of any importance—the *subjective* diminutive. It simply expressed the kindliness in her heart towards me and mine. We are not a sentimental people. I picked up a book of Yorkshire poems. Among them was an Ode to Spring. It began thus:

> T'aud Winter 'e got nawtice ter quit.
> He made sooch a muck o' the place.

I like to think that we Yorkshire people have another trait in common with the Russians. The vice we hate above all others is pretentiousness. I have heard one Russian charge another with pretentiousness; if it existed at all it was so infinitesimal as to be invisible to the naked English eye. Just so with the Yorkshireman. You may break every commandment of the Decalogue—he is easy enough, as long as you are a fairly good fellow he will pardon you—but try to show off, to impress him in any way, and you are done.

To such, I admit, my countrymen were cold and harsh. I remember a hapless clergyman who came north to take charge of our parish while the Vicar was away. The poor man arrived charged with good intentions; he meant to " brighten our Services "; he brought with him leaflets and new hymn-books and new hassocks to compel us to kneel flat upon our knees instead of comfortably crouching through the Litany as had been our Evangelical wont. He even put a little cross on the Communion Table, but this my father with his own hands swiftly and silently removed. The first Sunday the church was full; the second, spite of all the " brightness ", it was chill and empty save for a few sullen faces. I approved of the new man's views, though I did not like him, so I went conscientiously round to the chief parishioners to ask why they did not come to church. " We dawn't haud wi' 'is ways," was the answer. I thought it was the hassocks and the hymn-books and the leaflets. " Naw—'e could do as 'e liked wi' them papers and such like—they was naw matter—but we dawn't haud wi' 'is ways." Subsequent analysis taught me that " ways " is Yorkshire for the sum total of your reactions. Your particular deeds are of as little significance to him as your particular words; it is *you*, the whole of you, you "in a loomp", as he would say, that the Yorkshireman wisely reckons with. They were instinctively better bred than I was with my rationalising right and wrong, and they had felt the bad manners of the changes worked in their old Vicar's absence. After holding out for three months the innovator went back to his own place a sadder and a wiser Southerner.

My people must have been, I think, singularly old-fashioned and provincial even for those days. I remember that an old gentleman who came often to see us used to kiss my eldest sister's hand and call her "Mistress Elizabeth", unusual even in the 'fifties. How I wished some one would kiss my hand! But no one ever did till I came in my old age to courteous France. And as to Mistress Jane — no, it was Lady Jane I longed to be, for my cult was for Lady Jane Grey. I had a child's magical habit of mind; if I could get the name *exactly*, I should somehow possess the person. To name is to create. "And God said to the light, 'Light'" (He named it), and there *was* Light. So I consulted my kind nurse as to whether I could ever become Lady Jane. "Yes, of course, miss," said the cheery woman. "If you're good, maybe when you're a big girl you'll marry a lord and then you'll be a lady."

> Gentle Jane was as good as gold,
> She always did as she was told,
> And when she grew old, she was given in marriage
> To a first-class Earl who kept his carriage.

Hope shone bright, but I was a cautious child, and I referred the question to my better-informed governess. The blow fell. No, not even if I married a dozen lords could I ever be Lady Jane, unless they made my father an earl, which seemed somehow unlikely. So the dream faded, but not wholly. I could still " stay at home in my castle reading Plato while the ladies of the Court went hunting in the park ". And here I must confess my motives were not as purely platonic as they seem. The terror of my childhood was that I should be forced some day to ride to hounds. I loved the hounds, but oh how I hated the horses! I still hate their huge teeth and bulging eyes and satin skins. I learnt to ride (very badly) on an adorable donkey with long furry ears and soft kind eyes, and a small furry donkey slept in my bed every night for years. One night the nurse took it away, saying it was time I learnt not to be a baby. I said not a word, I had long learnt to keep silence.

But I was found at midnight with swollen eyes, staring wide awake. The nurse, being a sensible woman, put back my donkey, and I slept soft and warm. Alas! I was soon promoted to a Shetland pony, the veriest little imp of hell. He spent his time running away and buck-jumping; I spent my time prostrate on the Filey sands. He effectively broke my nerve; I was, and remain, a physical coward, and in a community of bold riders was an object of ignominy. No one understood, no one sympathised, till at a Swedish sanatorium I, by good fortune, met Mr. Lytton Strachey. We were both there to undergo Swedish massage, and Swedish massage as administered by a robust native is " no picnic ". " Take my advice," he said; " as soon as they touch you begin to yell, and go on yelling till they stop." It was sound advice, sympathetically given. I learnt then, for the first time, how tender, if how searching, is the finger Mr. Strachey lays on our human frailties.

My religious training was oddly mixed. My father was incapable of formulating a conviction, but I think he really would have sympathised with the eminent statesman who " had a great respect for religion as long as it did not interfere with a gentleman's private life!" I remember his look of annoyance when the Archbishop of York, who was lunching with us after a Confirmation, and had been told that I had played the village organ, put his hand on my head and bade me " consecrate my great gifts to God ". That Archbishop was a splendid figure to my childish imagination. I loved his ritual robes and voluminous sleeves, but one day I looked into my brother-in-law's study and found the apparitor arranging these vestments. Alas! the sleeves were not real sleeves, they came off. The apparitor, touched by my interest, very kindly showed me how they hooked on, but the gilt was off the gingerbread. To return to my father. The Archbishop was trying enough, but an old Evangelical clergyman was worse. He called to say good-bye to us one day and asked if, before parting, we would all kneel down and " ask a blessing " on our journey. I can see my father's face of cold disgust. He was in his own house and he could not be rude, so he sat down—he never knelt—and covered his angry face with one hand and let the old clergyman pray. Then he saw him courteously to the door and came back muttering something. I could only catch the word " indecent ". He attended church with fair regularity, but we children noticed that on

CHARLES HARRISON.

(Father of Jane Harrison.)

To face page 18.

what used to be called " Sacrament Sundays "
he was apt to have a slight attack of lumbago,
which passed off on Monday morning.

But my stepmother was made of quite
other metal. She was a Celt and her religion
was of the fervent semi-revivalist type. She
was a conscientious woman and tried to do
her duty, I am sure, to the three rather dour
little girls who had been her pupils and were
later presented to her as stepdaughters. She
gave us Scripture lessons every Sunday. Her
main doctrines were that we must be " born
again " and that " God would have our whole
hearts or nothing ". I think I early felt that
this was not quite fair. Why, if we were
to care for Him only, had He made this
delightful world full of enchanting foreign
languages? Anyhow, the holocaust I honestly
attempted was a complete failure. I was from
the outset a hopeless worldling. But the
apparatus of religion interested me. Sunday
was an exciting if laborious day. I taught
twice in the Sunday School, and from the
age of twelve played the organ at two services.
I followed the prayers in Latin, and the
lesson in German, and the Gospel in Greek;
this with some misgivings as to the " whole-
heartedness " of this proceeding. We always
had to write out one of the sermons from
memory, and were never told which. This

has given me a bad habit of attending closely to any nonsense I may happen to hear at a meeting or a lecture. I see my happier friends sleeping and yawning or nudging each other; my attention is glued to the speaker.

Every Sunday I learnt the Collect for the day and either the Epistle or the Gospel. My favourite Collect was that for Advent Sunday, and it still thrills me, but I cannot have had any real taste for literature as some of the hymns that delighted me most were abominable doggerel.

My favourite moral-song ran as follows:

> How proud we are, how pleased to show
> Our clothes and call them rich and new,
> When the poor sheep and silkworm wore
> That very clothing long before!

Partly, no doubt, it was that in my childish mind I had a pleasant picture of an old sheep suitably attired in a Victorian bonnet with strings and a shawl, but chiefly it pleased me because it expressed my innate and still inveterate dislike of, and contempt for, everything *chic* and smart. Perhaps it is some complex caused by my own childish sufferings in my " Sunday clothes ", though heaven knows they were plain enough. Anyhow, even now when I see a faultlessly turned out man or woman I always expect he or she will prove to be a fool and a bore. We cannot all be distinguished, but for heaven's sake let us all be shabby and comfortable. At a Cambridge function, when he was Chancellor, I once gazed with admiration at the late Duke of Devonshire. His right boot had a largish hole in it from which emerged a grey woollen toe. That, I felt, was really ducal. I turned the same sour eye on the very rich. I remember Miss Pernel Strachey raising the question: " Why do rich people always get so dull? " Now that Miss Strachey is Principal of Newnham, she will, I hope, employ some of her leisure in reading her Bible. " It is easier for a camel to go through a needle's eye than for a rich man to enter into the Kingdom of God." For " Kingdom of God " read " Kingdom of the higher spiritual values " and she has her answer.

My secular education till I was seventeen was in the hands of a rather rapid succession of governesses, all of them strictly English. My father's creed was a simple one: All foreigners were Papists, all Papists were liars, and he " wouldn't have one in his house ". How long and ardently I longed in vain to see a Papist! The result of my father's simple faith was that never in this world shall I be able to speak French. When I was sent to Cheltenham to be " finished ", I was placed in the Upper First at once because I could read three or four languages and knew " Noel et Chapsal " off by heart. My first morning the French master gave a simple *dictée*. Some isolated words I could make out, but not a single intelligible sentence. I sent in a blank sheet and cried with rage. All my governesses were grossly ignorant, but they were good women, steadily kind to me; they taught me deportment, how to come into a room, how to get into a carriage, also that " little girls should be seen and not heard ", and that I was there (in the schoolroom) " to learn, not to ask questions." On Saturdays we repeated the Books of the Bible in their correct order and the Kings of Israel and Judah, the signs of the Zodiac and the Tables of Weights and Measures. I also learnt by a mysterious system of mnemonics many isolated dates. I can still give correctly the date of the Creation of the World, the Fall, the Flood, the battle of Quebec and the Discovery of the Circulation of the Blood.

Victorian education was ingeniously useless. Every day I spent an hour doing exquisite hems and seams. I cannot to this day make the simplest garment. But for some things I am devoutly thankful. I was made to learn for some fifteen years three verses of the Bible every day. I might choose what poetry I wished. In this way I learnt impartially great quantities of Milton, Wordsworth and Mrs. Hemans, Gray's "Elegy", the "Prisoner of Chillon" and the like. I learnt them all lying on a back-board, and to this day my flat back is the admiration of dressmakers. When, nowadays, I see the round backs of my young friends, and watch them slinking round doors as though they were criminals and not English gentlewomen, and especially when they fail to get up when addressed by their elders and betters, I sometimes sigh for a little "deportment", but, after all, we of a past generation have no more right to impose our manners than we have to impose our morals. When a young man comes to tea with me for the first time, it gives me, I confess, a slight shock when he lies down full length on the rug, but thereby he expresses his willingness for a kindly relation, and things are more comfortable than if he sat, hat in hand, on the edge of his chair. Again, it surprised me a little when at Cambridge I asked a young man to tea for the first time and he answered *on a post-card*: "I'll come if I can, but don't count on me." "Count on" him, the lout! I crossed his name (an honoured name by the by) out of my address book, but the same evening—in penance for my bad temper—I wrote to him *on a post-card* and said I hoped I might " count on him " for another Sunday. And then things change so swiftly; the vulgarism of one generation is the polished *cliché* of the next. When I was young, to apologise by saying " sorry " would have been —witness the *Punch* of the period—to write yourself down a shop-man; now I hear " sorry " drop quite easily from the most blue-blooded lips. As to the absurdities of Victorian education, we learnt certainly a great deal of miscellaneous rubbish (I am prepared though to defend the signs of the Zodiac), but odd scraps of information are stimulating to a child's imagination. Nowadays it seems you learn only what is reasonable and relevant. I went to Rome with a young friend, educated on the latest lines, and who had taken historical honours at Cambridge. The first morning the pats of butter came up stamped with the Twins. " Good old Romulus and Remus," said I. " Good old who? " said she. She had never heard of the Twins and was much bored when I told her the story; they had no place in " constitutional history ", and for her the old wolf of the Capitol howled in vain: " Great God! I'd rather be . . ."

We old people must, however, steadily face the fact that the young are more likely to be right than the old, and this in literature as in morals and manners. If we old ones have behind us a larger personal experience, they, the young, have behind them the collective experience of a whole additional generation. Youth starts life from the vantage point of the shoulders of age, and his vista is likely to be wider and clearer. As Mr. Sheppard observed: " When the fathers think that the Age of Reason is achieved, the sons may be trusted, if they are of good stock, to see that it is still far off." I will make a personal confession. The methods of the Georgian novelist have often tried me sorely. I had always been used to think of art as a thing of selection. I looked to it for a certain peace and largeness. Then when I took up " Ulysses ", I found myself not only wallowing in a drain of obscenities that would have abashed Zola, but also exposed to a trickle of trivialities that exasperated my every nerve, and made me feel as though I were in a psycho-analyst's consulting room with a patient forced to unburden himself of every thought, every impression, however feeble and seemingly irrelevant. And yet all the time I felt, " This is written by a man of genius, who am I to judge him? Let me try first to understand him." " Psycho-analyst's consulting room." Yes, the conviction grew. Joyce is trying to make audible, make conscious the subconscious. He is dredging the great deeps of personality. That is his tremendous contribution, and after him follow a host of less-gifted imitators. Then, happily, I read *Mr. Bennett and Mrs. Brown,* and Mrs. Woolf made me see that these Georgian characters, which I had thought were so unreal and even teasing, were real with an intimacy and a spirituality before unattempted. So I have my reward. I don't say I always get there! I don't say that when I go joyously to bed with a novel, it is Mr. Joyce I take with me. It is not, it is Jane Austen or George Eliot or even Trollope, but at least I know there is somewhere to get to; the gates of a New Jerusalem are even for me ajar!

To return to my governesses. There was one notable exception—a woman of real intelligence, ignorant but willing and eager to learn anything and everything I wanted. Together we learnt to read German, Latin badly, and with the quantities of course all wrong, the Greek Testament and even a little Hebrew. Unfortunately, having no guide, we began with the Psalms which are hard nuts to crack. I wanted to find out the meaning of such obscure and exciting verses as " Or ever your pots be made hot with thorns, so let indignation vex him even as a thing that is raw ". Alas! my kind governess was shortly removed to a lunatic asylum. What share I may have had in her mental downfall I do not care to inquire.

A keen impulse was given to my study of the Greek Testament by the arrival of a new curate. He was fresh from Oxford and not, I think, averse to showing off. Rashly in one of his sermons he drew attention to a mis-translation. This filled me with excitement and alarm. I saw in a flash that the whole question of the " verbal inspiration of the Bible " was at issue. That afternoon I took my Greek Testament down to the Sunday School and, eager for further elucidation, waylaid the hapless curate. I soon found that his know-ledge of Greek was, if possible, more slender than my own. But, if embarrassed, he was friendly. Alas! that curate did not confine his attentions to the Greek text. I was summarily despatched in dire disgrace to Cheltenham. My stepmother said I was behaving "like a kitchen-maid". Consider-ing the subject of my converse with the curate, I fail to see the analogy. My father, as usual, said nothing. He scarcely ever did say anything. His great natural silence—

which he has handed down to me—was, I think, increased by my stepmother's rather violent Celtic volubility. "Mother'd talk the hind leg off a donkey," observed one of her sons. I heard her voice once in an adjoining room passionately haranguing my father. From him not a sound. But when we met for dinner, we saw with some embarrassment that a portrait of my mother, long consigned to an attic, was hanging on the wall opposite my father's seat. He had himself brought it down and hung it up. Such was his dumb reprisal. My mother died almost at my birth, but I have been told she was a silent woman of singular gentleness and serenity.

Books were, till I went to school, a serious difficulty. My father's school-books had somehow perished. I saved up my money to buy a second-hand Virgil. The process was long, for my income was sixpence a week, mulcted of a compulsory penny for the missionaries. My edition of the *Aeneid* contained not a hint as to scansion. I knew the poem was in hexameters, but I was constantly held up by the elision of nasal terminations. I was almost in despair when a boy-friend who had just been promoted to doing verse at school offered to show me, as he expressed it, " how to do the trick ". His explanations were a veritable Apocalypse and I was enraptured,

ELIZABETH HAWKSLEY HARRISON (*née* NELSON).

(Mother of Jane Harrison.)

To face page 28.

but he rather let me down by observing at the end, " It's a silly game, but if you're in the Fourth you've got to do it ! "

This same boy-friend got me into serious disgrace later at school, at Cheltenham. I was working for the London Matriculation then just opened to women, and he proposed to write to me just before the examination to " buck me up ". No letter reached me, but one morning I was summoned before Miss Beale's throne, where she sat in state before the Lower School came into prayers. She had in front of her a post-card (post-cards had only just been invented) written in a schoolboy scrawl and signed " Peveril ". " That ", she said, pointing a disgusted finger at the signature, " is a boy's name." " Yes," I said, " it's Peveril; he promised to write to me before the examination," and I put out my hand for the post-card. " No, this must go to your parents," and then came a long harangue. It ended with these words which intrigued me so that I remember them exactly: " You are too young, and I hope too innocent, to realise the gross vulgarity of such a letter or the terrible results to which it might lead." I was indeed, and still am, for what do you think was the offence? After his signature " Peveril " had written " *Give my love to the Examiners!* " The story may stand to mark the abyss of fatuous prudery into which the girls' schools of the middle Victorian period— even the very best—had fallen. I was too furious that my letter had been read to think of anything else. At home a scrupulous code of honour prevailed as to letters. I remember being allowed to take a bundle of letters to the village post. I employed my time learning by heart the various names, titles, prefixes and addresses. These when I got back I repeated, expecting praise for my diligence and accuracy. Instead I was told I had done a most dishonourable thing. Never, under any circumstances, was I to read the address of a letter unless addressed to myself. *Tempora mutantur.* I know a certain distinguished family all of whose members make a practice of reading all post-cards and all the letters left lying about the house. When I got home, my father sent for me and said, " Miss Beale said I was to read that," pointing to the post-card. " I don't see any harm in it—but he'd no business to write to you on a post-card, the puppy." Post-cards were an innovation and all innovations anathema. All boys and all young men who proposed for his daughters were to my father " puppies ". It is only due to " Peveril " to add that this offence he never committed, hence much was forgiven him. Peveril is a county magnate now, a Justice of

the Peace, a Constant Reader of the *Spectator*
—not, I feel sure, of the *Nation*!

I, too, am a Justice of the Peace. I
mention this not as an empty boast, but in all
humility, because my short experience as a
magistrate taught me much. I should like
every young man and woman to go through
this experience for a year or two and not wait
till they are sixty and it is too late to become
a good citizen. I may say at once that I was
quite useless on the Bench. I have really no
head for business, and am prone to observe
only the irrelevant. A candid friend told me
that I had been chosen just " to represent Art
and Letters ", and that *therefore* only an
elegant indolence was expected of me. Still,
I like to remember that I saved a poor
Armenian from a fine. He had somehow
muddled his identity card. I felt that all
consideration was due to any one who could
speak Armenian, perhaps the most difficult of
all European languages. And then, what
about my own identity card? A very moderate
amount of red tape is apt to make me " see
red ", but I can just manage to fill in a passport
form and describe my eyes, my nose, my fore-
head and my figure generally, but when the
préfecture asks for the birthplace of your
maternal grandfather, what are you to do?

If you speak the truth and say you don't know
and don't want to, you will be detained at the
pleasure of the Republic, stand for hours in
a queue of Polish Jews and get no lunch.
The only sound policy is to write in the name
of some obscure Yorkshire village. As the
official will not be able to read, still less to
pronounce it, his official soul will be satisfied.
This, I fancy, was what the Armenian had
been after. Anyhow, I got him off.

We had, of course, dull hours—mainly
spent in fining undergraduates for exceeding
speed limits. If you have been knocked down
twice yourself, at first you feel a ferocious
joy, but vengeance soon palls. As a rule no
attempt was made at defence; the under-
graduate had had his fun and cheerfully paid
down his—or rather his father's—money
in fines of ever-increasing severity. One
brighter spirit, I remember, began a long and
laboured defence; it was couched in a lingo
unknown to me, some strange up-to-date
slang. I began eagerly to take valuable
linguistic notes. But the presiding magistrate
was a cold insensate man, dead to the charms
of language; he curtly requested the under-
graduate to confine his remarks to the King's
English. The poor boy looked round piteously,
said, " Yes, sir ; thank you, sir," and
collapsed.

Many of the charges were for petty thefts. At first this embarrassed me a good deal. I could not bear to look at the prisoner lest he should be suffering agonies of shame. I soon found my embarrassment was needless. Shame is the high prerogative of a sensitive humanity. These poor creatures were not shameless because they were hardened criminals; they were just too stupid to feel shame. They were, most of them, morally half-witted, cases not for the law, but the leech or the psychologist. One pitiable case I remember of a man more intelligent but slightly maudlin. We had to examine into his wretched past. He told us of his hopeless efforts to get work, of occasional jobs lost through drink, petty thefts and the like. For years he had drifted lower and lower. "Then", said he, "came the war. That *was* a bit of luck. I got a job at once and kept it, and then", he added sadly, "came the bluggy Peace and they chucked me." No criticism, I am sure, was intended of the high conventions of Versailles, it was just that he had lost his job. I think all the Bench hung their heads. This was the world as we, its rulers, had made it.

Let no one think that the English Bench is a place unfit for a lady. One day it was reported by the constable that the prisoner had used peculiarly foul language. "What did he say?" asked a magistrate. "Well, sir, it isn't hardly fit for me to repeat," said the constable. The clerk added that he had had the "language" typed and a copy would be handed round if the Bench desired. The Bench did desire, and it was circulated. The unknown to me has always had an irresistible lure, and all my life I have had a curiosity to know what really bad language consisted of. In the stables at home I had heard an occasional "damn" from the lips of a groom, but that was not very informing. Now was the chance of my life. The paper reached the old gentleman next me. I had all but stretched out an eager hand. He bent over me in a fatherly way and said, "I am sure *you* will not want to see this." I was pining to read it, but sixty years of sex-subservience had done their work. I summoned my last blush, cast down my eyes and said, "O no! No. Thank you so much." Elate with chivalry he bowed and pocketed the script.

I have always known we English were a good-natured, easy-going people, serenely sure of ourselves, not prone to take offence, but on the Bench I learnt that we are something a little more. Every official, from the presiding magistrate to the constable, had for the prisoner a steady courtesy and a real consideration and even kindliness. Once only did I hear a barrister begin to bluster a little and slightly heckle a prisoner, but the feeling of the court was so manifestly against him that he swiftly collapsed. There was to be no bullying of the under dog.

But all this is by anticipation. To return to Cheltenham. I had to face the ordeal of the Matriculation Examination of the London University, uncheered by " Peveril's " letter. Examinations were novelties then. I felt the whole honour of the College was on my shoulders and I was almost senseless from nervousness. To my dying day I shall affectionately remember the Registrar of the University. Before I went in he asked my name. I could not remember it. Everything had gone blank. He looked at me so kindly and said, " Oh it is of no consequence, later on perhaps." And later he came into the Hall to see how I was getting on. He found me writing merrily.

I carried away from Cheltenham College a dislike for history which has lasted all my life. Our history lessons consisted mainly in moralisings on the doings and misdoings of kings and nobles. We did the Stuart period in tedious detail, and as Miss Beale was Cromwellian and I, like all children, a passionate Royalist, I was in a constant state of irritation.   There was an odd rule through-out the College that no girl might buy a book. It sprang from Miss Beale's horror of what she called " undigested knowledge ".   She need not have feared with most of us that the amount of knowledge absorbed, digested or undigested, would have been excessive.   I broke the rule and secretly bought a small life of Archbishop Laud.   This I read, learned, marked and inwardly digested.   Later, I again broke the rule and bought Bryce's *Holy Roman Empire*.   Mr. Bryce was coming to examine us and I scored handsomely by my perfidy.   Normally, what we had to feed on were the notes we took of lectures; these notes were carefully corrected and severely commented on.   It was a wretched starvation system, but gave constant practice in com-position.   For two things, however, I am thankful to Cheltenham.   Arithmetic and elementary mathematics were admirably taught, and it was a rapture to me to understand at last why you turned fractions upside down in division.   When I first got possession of an x I felt I had a new mastery of the world. Only my teachers stopped short too soon—just where real mathematics began, and when later at Cambridge I heard Mr. Bertrand Russell discourse on the amazing beauty of mathematics, I felt like a Peri outside Paradise.

I had no mathematical ability. I never saw the inner necessity of the truths of which I wrote the proofs with glib understanding, but my teachers might have dragged me through at least the Calculuses.

But, most of all, I am grateful for my training in elementary chemistry. We had lectures with experiments, and a few of us were allowed to go and do analyses of simple substances at the laboratory of the boys' college. You watch an experiment, some one pours some hydrosulphuric acid (I hope it *is* hydrosulphuric acid, my chemistry is faded) on some loaf sugar, and in a moment the quiet white sugar is a seething black volcano. Things are never the same to you again. You know they *are* not what they seem; you picture hidden terrific forces, you can even imagine that the whole solid earth is only such forces held in momentous balance.

Though I have lived most of my life with educationalists, I have little interest in education. I dislike schools, both for boys and girls. A child between the ages of eight and eighteen, the normal school years, is too young to form a collective opinion, children only set up foolish savage taboos. I dislike also all plans for " developing a child's mind ", and all conscious forms of personal influence of the younger by the elder. Let children early speak at least three foreign languages, let them browse freely in a good library, see all they can of the first-rate in nature, art, and literature—above all, give them a chance of knowing what science and scientific method means, and then leave them to sink or swim. Above all things, do not cultivate in them a taste for literature.

In answer to numerous inquiries, I beg to state that my first literary effort was a tract entitled " Praying for Rain ". I was in urgent need of a guinea to subscribe to a portrait of Miss Beale and I dared not ask for such a sum. I sent my attempt to the Religious Tract Society and almost by return came back a post-office order for three guineas. If I had kept to tract-writing, I would not be the needy woman I still am. I shall never forget the sight of that delicious thin green paper. It was to me untold wealth, but I was burdened with a sense of guilt. I dared not tell my father about the post-office order. He held old-fashioned views as to women earning money. To do so was to bring disgrace on the men of the family. I longed to spend the extra two guineas on books, but I dared not. Long ago I had told a lie and been made to stay at home from Church and learn by heart the story of Ananias and Sapphira, who *kept*

38

back part of the price. " The feet of the young men who carried them out " seemed to be waiting for me, so I offered my holocaust, sent the whole three guineas to Miss Beale's portrait, and thereby, I hope, effaced the blot from the family scutcheon. I always sent a copy of every book I wrote to my father, and he always acknowledged them in the same set words: " Thank you for the book you have sent me, your mother and sisters are well. Your affectionate father." I am sure he never read them, and I suspect his feeling towards them was what the Freudians call *ambivalent*—half shame, half pride. Years after his death I learnt, and it touched me deeply, that, on the rare occasions when he left home, he took with him a portmanteau full of my books. Why? Well, after all, he was a Yorkshireman, it may have been he wanted a "bit o' coompany".

My father was the shyest man I ever knew, and terribly absent-minded. Legend says that two years after he was married he rode up to Limber Grange, my maternal grandfather's house, and asked to see Miss Elizabeth Nelson. I know myself that if he found unexpected visitors in the drawing-room, he would give a frightened look round, shake hands courteously with his embarrassed wife and daughters, and disappear like a shot deer.

In our rambling, uncomfortable old house he had furnished for himself a Harbour of Refuge, known as his workroom. It contained countless fishing-rods and a lathe on which he turned boxes of ebony and ivory. It would have been a bold servant who would have intruded there; even my stepmother dare not enter unbidden. My father always said grace before dinner and luncheon, but was furious when a clerical son-in-law wanted to say it before breakfast. The form he adopted, and from which nothing could wean him, was his own: " For what we are about to receive, *may the Lord be truly thankful.*" My own absences of mind I control severely, but I have occasional lapses, as when I turned into the trimming of a white muslin tennis hat three ten pound notes destined to pay my college fees. Six months later, after much fruitless and anguished searching, the trimming was unpicked and the notes emerged.

My elder sister was less successful. As a clergyman's wife, it was part of her frequent duty to write " characters " for young parishioners seeking situations. Every college tutor at the end of the May-term knows the suffering entailed. Any form of literary composition caused my sister acute agony. One day my niece and I noticed that she was sitting at her writing-table with the characteristic hunted look. " I wonder what old Dobbin is up to," said my niece. (Old Dobbin was her reverent appellation for a really adored mother.) "Writing testimonials by the look of her," said I. " I'll go and look," said my niece. Looking over her mother's shoulder, my niece read, " I am seeking a situation for a young cat, Mr. Velvet Brown (the actual name of my small nephew's cat, at the time felt to be superfluous). I can in every way heartily recommend him; he is a good mouser, affectionate and clean in person and habits. He has lived for some months in a clergyman's family." Here she paused, pen in air, for inspiration, and was gradually restored to reality by a prolonged giggle.

I ought, in justice to my sister, to explain that " Mr. Velvet Brown " played a large part in the home life of the Vicarage, which he never left till death removed him. He was a cat of great dignity. Tail in air, he always trotted after my brother-in-law on his parish rounds. If he was lost the whole house was upset. My small nephew was, after the fashion of his generation, usually kind and forbearing to his mother. I remember once she was, I must own, rather " nagging " at him, and he said to her gently, " There, there, Mother, that will do." But when my sister

said angrily, " Where on earth has that cat
got to? " he looked at her reprovingly and
answered, " Mother, Mr. Velvet Brown has
gone for a stroll; he will be back for supper,
and you'd better keep some fish and a saucer of
cream." One of my most cherished posses-
sions is a photograph I still have of Mr.
Velvet Brown. He is taken standing on his
hind-legs with his right paw uplifted. This
was supposed to be my brother-in-law's
favourite pulpit attitude. But, alas! Mr.
Velvet Brown was not what the French call
" un chat sérieux ", and one evening he went
out to return no more. It was this absence
of mind in my sister and not, as I then stupidly
thought, lack of brains that made her constru-
ing of Latin sometimes fail to carry conviction.
I can hear her musical voice now, as she
stumbled through the dreary waste of a Latin
exercise book. " The sharp horse was prick-
ing on the idle spur." Her wits were always
wool-gathering like my father's, and here was
no wool to gather. I would not " put it
past " her now to assert that " the wall was
building up Balbus ".

My father left Yorkshire because of the
threatened approach within a mile of our house
of a small branch railway, connecting Scarbro'
and Whitby. He feared it would bring with
it tourists, char-à-bancs, gas lighting, and all

the pollution of villadom. I think he was unduly anxious. We left, but about ten years later I came back on a visit to friends. I had occasion to go down to the little moorland station to fetch a parcel of books. The tiny train came puffing up, stopped; the guard's van opened and some parcels were flung out. Then forth stepped the single passenger, a great grey sheep-dog, respectfully met by the station-master. Yorkshire is a Paradise for dogs, specially sporting dogs. I have seen them crowding the platform at York station about the Twelfth of August, waited on assiduously by eager porters while their masters went neglected. But all dogs are treated with due respect. I was once privileged to attend a huge St. Bernard on his way home from Yorkshire. My friend and I travelled first-class in honour of our great companion. The guard looked at the three of us, grinned, and said, "Happen t'awd dog ud liever not travel wi' strangers." He clapped an "Engaged" on the carriage and was gone, never waiting for or, I am sure, thinking of a tip.

CHAPTER II

CAMBRIDGE AND LONDON

AT Cambridge great men and women began
to come into my life. Women's colleges were
a novelty, and distinguished visitors were
brought to see us as one of the sights. Turgenev
came, and I was told off to show him round.
It was a golden opportunity. Dare I ask
him to speak just a word or two of Russian?
He looked such a kind old snow-white Lion.
Alas! he spoke fluent English; it was a
grievous disappointment. Then Ruskin came.
I showed him our small library. He looked
at it with disapproving eyes. " Each book ",
he said gravely, " that a young girl touches
should be bound in white vellum." I thought
with horror of the red moroccos and Spanish
leather that had been my choice. A few
weeks later the old humbug sent us his own
works bound in dark blue calf! Then came
Mr. Gladstone. His daughter Helen was a
college friend of mine, or rather, more

JANE HARRISON (aged twenty-five).

To face page 45.

exactly, a friendly enemy. We fought about everything, and had not an idea in common. She was the most breezy, boisterous creature possible; we called her Boreas, for she had a habit of picking her friends up and running with them the length of the corridors. She was a thorough Lyttelton, without a trace of her father, whom she adored. I was a rigid Tory in those days, and I resolutely refused to join the mob of students in cheering and clapping the Grand Old Man on his arrival. I shut myself up in my room. Thither—to tease me —she brought him. He sat down and asked me who was my favourite Greek author. Tact counselled Homer, but I was perverse and not quite truthful, so I said "Euripides." Æschylus would have been creditable, Sophocles respectable, but the sceptic Euripides! It was too much, and with a few words of warning he withdrew. And then last, but oh, so utterly first, came George Eliot. It was in the days when her cult was at its height—thank heaven I never left her shrine!—and we used to wait outside Macmillan's shop to seize the new instalments of *Daniel Deronda*. She came for a few minutes to my room, and I was almost senseless with excitement. I had just repapered my room with the newest thing in dolorous Morris papers. Some one must have called her attention to it, for I remember that she said in her shy, impressive way, " Your paper makes a beautiful background for your face." The ecstasy was too much, and I knew no more. Later, in London, I met, of course, many eminent men, but there never came again a moment like that. Browning was only to me a cheerful, amusing gossip. Herbert Spencer took me in to dinner once, but he would discuss the Athenæum cook, and on that subject he found me ill-informed. Pater and his sisters were good, and opened their house to me; I always think of him as a soft, kind cat; he purred so persuasively that I lost the sense of what he was saying. At his house I often met Henry James. I liked to watch that ingenious spider weaving his webs, but to me he had no appeal. Miss Bosanquet's recent delightful *Henry James at Work* has made me realise what I lost.

Tennyson's daughter-in-law, Mrs. Lionel Tennyson, later Mrs. Augustine Birrell, was among my closest friends. She took me to stay with the great man. He met us at the station, grunting fiercely that he " was not going to dress for dinner because I had come." It was rather frightening, but absurd. The vain old thing (he was the most openly vain man I ever met) knew quite well that he looked his best in his ample poet's cloak. It is a rare and austere charm that gains by evening dress. He was very kind to me according to his rather fierce lights; he took me a long, memorable Sunday morning walk, recited "Maud" to me, and countless other things. It was an anxious joy; he often forgot his own poems and was obviously annoyed if I could not supply the words. He would stop suddenly and ask angrily: "Do you think Browning could have written that line? Do you think Swinburne could?" I could truthfully answer, "Impossible." If he posed a good deal, he was scarcely to blame; the house was so charged with an atmosphere of hero-worship that free breathing was difficult. Tennyson remains to me a great poet, and I am proud to have known him. When I hear young reactionaries say he is no poet at all, I think them simply silly. He was intensely English, and therefore not at his best as a conscious thinker; but he felt soundly, and his mastery of language was superb. While the English language is, such poems as "In Memoriam", "The Lotus-Eaters", "Ulysses", "Crossing the Bar" must live. Of very great artists there were, in England, none to know. But I learnt much from the young school of Impressionists then fighting their way to recognition. Burne-Jones too was kind to me; he used often to come and sit with me, turning over drawings of Greek vases with eager, delighted fingers. Sometimes I sat with him as he drew his strange visions; often a silent, decorative cat sat on his shoulder. He wrote me many letters with whimsical illustrative drawings. I am sorry now that I tore them up. The people I most longed after, Christina Rossetti and Swinburne, were not diners-out, and I never knew them. The men and women who influenced me most —my real friends—are living still. Of them I may not write.

One dear, dead woman remains—Miss Thackeray, who later married Richmond Ritchie, the brother of a college friend. I met her first at Eton, and I like to think she took a fancy to me, for she asked me down to Chiswick to see her. She suggested an afternoon, at five, and at five I presented myself. She received me with open arms, and hospitably put her hand on a small black satin bag in which I carried my book for the train. " Let Susan take your luggage upstairs," she said. " Come and have tea." I clung to the said " luggage ", and explained that she had not asked me to stay the night. " Oh, but I want you to stay a long, long time." Why, oh why, did I not stay? Was it that I shrank from breaking a dinner engagement, or was it a snobbish fear that Susan, as she unpacked my " luggage ", might think a copy of Christina Rossetti's poems inadequate night-gear? I lost my opportunity, she never asked me again. I met her soon after, crossing Kensington Square; she shook hands, but seemed excited and *affairée*. " I mustn't stop; some friends—some dear, dear friends —are coming to dinner, and I have promised to get them an egg." And she was gone to the High Street. She never, I think, had her delicate feet quite on the ground. I have often been sorry that I did not keep *Punch's* fine parody of her novels. It ended thus: " A kind hand was outstretched to help me. Two kind hands. I never knew which I took."

Walter Raleigh was an early friend, he and his delightful mother and sisters. I remember we were all sitting round the fire after dinner one night, and Walter was reading out some of his verses. One poem was about the on-coming of Night and contained the line:

And God leads round His starry Bear.

" How beautiful! " I murmured fatuously (my friends tell me that at any mention of a bear I am apt to get maudlin). " Walter," said his mother fiercely, " how dare you be so blasphemous! God doesn't lead round bears." "Well, mother," said Walter, "it's your fault; you always used to tell us when we were children that God guided the stars in their paths, and ", looking at me, "I learnt it all at my mother's knee." "I am sure your father wouldn't have liked it," continued his mother. At this appeal to his filial piety Walter, of course, collapsed, but he told me afterwards, in private, that he was sure his father would have liked the line about the Bear, and that he should keep it in. Dr. Raleigh, it seems, held unusually wide views for a Congregationalist minister. Mrs. Raleigh was always called in her family "Mrs. Fox", because of the unexpected whiskings of her mind. When the British Government broke out into a sort of epidemic of title-giving, confounding gentlemen and scholars with lord mayors and profiteers, Walter was of course knighted. I had scarcely a friend left who was not so mishandled. His family were amused and rather disgusted, but Walter himself was simply delighted and played with his absurd title like a toy. Smart ladies began to take him up and pet him, and his sisters called him " the duchesses' darling ", but he just genuinely enjoyed it all. He was the one plain son in a family of extraordinarily handsome daughters, all " variations ", as some one said, " of a beautiful theme ". But though he was plain to uncouthness as a young man, all through his life some unseen inner spirit was at work, chiselling his face, and, before he died, he was beautiful. He was the best talker I ever knew, and a quite inspired lecturer. The views he tenaciously held were reactionary and, to my mind, preposterous. We wrangled ceaselessly. He paid, alas, for his fantastic militarism with his life.

In those days I met many specimens of a class of Victorian who, if not exactly distinguished, were at least distinctive and are, I think, all but extinct—British Lions and Lionesses. The Lionesses first—that was the name we gave them at Newnham. They were all spinsters, well-born, well-bred, well-educated and well off. They attended my lectures on Greek Art. Greek Art was at that time booming and was eminently respectable. At home they gardened a great deal; they, most of them, had country houses. Their gardens were a terror to me, for I never could remember the names of the plants with slips attached to them, and to blunder over a plant's name was as bad to a Lioness as a false quantity. They kept diaries in which they entered accurately the state of the weather on each day. If they lived in London they promoted Friendly Girls and Workhouse Nursing. Above all, they kept a vigilant eye on the shortcomings of local officials; they frequently wrote to the *Times*, heading their letters: "*Re* Mud and Slush". In the spring and early summer they went to Italy, accompanied usually by "a young relative", whose expenses they paid; they voyaged mainly to Rome and Florence, but the more adventurous went to Assisi. Attired in mushroom hats, veils and dust cloaks, they sketched a great deal. The subject of their sketches was always recognisable—ruined towers and church porches. The ordinary man was to them negligible, but they spoke of their own male relatives with respect and frequently quoted the opinions of " my uncle, the Dean ", or " my cousin, the Archdeacon ". They were a fine upstanding breed, and I miss them. They had no unsatisfied longings, had never heard of " suppressed complexes ", and lived happily their vigorous, if somewhat angular, lives.

Their counterparts were the British Lions. Of them, naturally, I knew less. Real intimacy between the two genders was not in those days usual, but I watched them with delight from afar. You could always count on them to roar suitably. I worked for some

time on the Council of the Girls' Public Day
School Company, which was largely manned
by British Lions, and I was privileged to go
with them to preside at local prize-givings.
They made speeches and I held a large and
agonising bouquet. The sentiments of these
speeches were on well-established lines, and
always, always, at the end came the in-
evitable:

> A perfect woman, nobly planned
> To warn, to comfort, and command.

I thought at one time of offering a small
prize of half-a-crown to any Lion who would
resist that temptation. A little later I worked
on the Council of the Classical Association.
There I might safely have raised the prize
to five shillings. There lived no Lion who
could end his address without telling you that
it was the writing of Latin Prose that had
made him what he was! Am I indiscreet
if I mention that I was yachting once with
a British Lion? He was oldish and had a
deck-cabin. I happened to look in in passing.
On the table lay a Bible, on the Bible a tooth-
brush. Cleanliness was " next to godliness ".
Oh England—my England!

It was about then that I began lecturing
on Greek Art at boys' schools. Archdeacon

Wilson first asked me to Clifton; he told me afterwards that he had not dared to tell his Council that the lecturer was a woman till all was over. Later I learnt that among my audience had been no less persons than Dr. MacTaggart and Roger Fry, and that they had deigned to discuss my lecture. Then Mr. Warre Cornish, always the kindest of friends, asked me to Eton. I do not suppose the lectures did any good, but they amused the boys. One of the masters asked a very small Winchester "man" if he had liked the lecture. "Not the lecture," he said candidly, "but I liked the lady; she was like a beautiful green beetle." In those days one's evening gowns were apt to be covered with spangles, and mine of blue-green satin had caught the light of the magic-lantern. A young prig, who bore an honoured name, was introduced to me at Eton; he wrote me next day a patronising letter of thanks, in which he said he hoped to go on with archæology, as he was going up to Oxford to "do Grates". Alas! he never *did* anything half so useful. My youngest brother was at Harrow; he wrote to me to say he had heard I was lecturing at Eton. It didn't matter, apparently, what I did at that benighted place, but he "did hope I wasn't coming lecturing at Harrow, as it would make

JANE HARRISON (aged thirty-three).

To face page 54.

it very awkward for him with the other fellows." I saw his position and respected it.

Then there was the actual Cambridge Academic circle—a brilliant circle, it seems to me, looking back. Cambridge society was then small enough to be one, and there were endless small, but not informal, dinner-parties. The order of University precedence was always strictly observed. Henry Sidgwick was the centre, and with him his two most intimate friends, Frederick Myers and Edmund Gurney. Frederick Myers rang, perhaps, the most sonorously of all, but to me he always rang a little false. Edmund Gurney was, I think, the most lovable and beautiful human being I ever met. This was the Psychical Research circle; their quest, scientific proof of immortality. To put it thus seems almost grotesque now; then it was inspiring. About this nucleus from a wider world ranged Balfours, Jebbs, and later rose a younger generation—the three Darwin sons, the Verralls, husband and wife, both my closest friends; Robert Neil of Pembroke, whose sympathetic Scotch silences made the dreariest gathering burn and glow; the George Protheros, Frederick Maitland, whose daughter, Fredegond Shove, is now the sweetest of our lyrical singers. And in the midst of them Mrs. Henry Sidgwick (the younger Miss Balfour) shone like a star. She had none of her husband's or her brother's social gifts, yet in any society she shone with a sort of lambent light. When we took her for our Principal, I am afraid science lost a fine researcher. Still, she had a perfect passion for accounts. "Why need I dress for dinner," she said to me plaintively, "when I might be getting on with these?" touching her account-books tenderly. She was meticulously true. We were talking once in Hall of the odd lingo that shops and business invent, "haberdashery", "hosiery", etc.—words unknown to the outside world. I cited, "*Alight* here for the Albert Memorial". Whoever says "alight"? "I always say 'alight'," remarked Mrs. Sidgwick; "it's a very good word." "Forgive me," said I "I'm quite sure you don't." A few minutes later she joined me in the corridor. "You are quite right," she said; "I find I don't say 'alight' but", cautiously, "I think I always shall now." I do hope she does! Another time I was holding forth on the supreme importance of classics in education. "Don't you think", she said, "you a little confuse between the importance of your subject and the extraordinary delight you manage to extract from it?" That was well observed. Her great truthfulness made her very naïve; she walked through a vulgar and wicked world in perpetual blinkers. Though her austerity of dress and manners always made me feel a vulgarian, how I adored her! how she made me laugh! I never told my love, and, alas! on college politics I had almost always to oppose her. Sheltered by the publicity of *The Nation* I tell it now. Why is it that those we most adore most move us to mirth? As soon as we laugh at a person we begin a little to love them.

One scientific friend, Francis Darwin, had lasting influence on me. Classics he regarded with a suspicious eye, but he was kind to me. One day he found me busy writing an article on the " Mystica vannus Iacchi ". " I must get it off to-night," I said industriously. " What is a *vannus?* " he asked. " Oh, a ' fan '," I said; " it was a mystical object used in ceremonies of initiation." " Yes, but Virgil says it is an agricultural implement. Have you ever seen one? " " No," I confessed. " *And you are writing about a thing you have never seen,*" groaned my friend. " Oh, you classical people! " It did not end there. He interviewed farmers— no result; he wrote to agricultural institutes abroad, and, finally, in remote provincial France, unearthed a mystic " fan " still in use, and had it despatched to Cambridge. Luckily he also found that his old gardener was perhaps the last man in England who could use the obsolete implement. On his lawn were to be seen a gathering of learned scholars trying, and failing, to winnow with the *vannus*. Its odd shape explained all its uses, mystic and otherwise. Three months later I despatched a paper to the *Hellenic Journal* on what I *had* seen and *did* understand. It was a lifelong lesson to me. It was not quite all my fault. I had been reared in a school that thought it was far more important to parse a word than to understand it. I had myself, as a student, eagerly asked why the *vannus* was mystic, and the answer had been, " You have construed the passage correctly; that will do for the present." And as my " coach " closed his Virgil, he remarked sadly, " Bad sport in subjunctives to-day." Such training was perhaps the best possible for my always flighty mind.

The last distinguished person whom I helped to entertain years later, at Newnham, was the Crown Prince of Japan. If you must curtsey to a man young enough to be your grandson, it is at least some consolation to know that he believes himself to be God. It was that which interested me. I found in the

Prince a strange charm. He was intensely quiet and had about him a sort of serenity and security that really seemed divine. Japanese is one of the few languages which contain the hard *i*. All Indo-European languages have lost it, except Russian, though a Russian told me that he had heard the exact sound from the lips of a cockney newspaper boy pronouncing " Piccad*i*lly ". The Prince was good enough to say his own royal name to me two or three times, but alas! I forgot it.

My lot has not lain in the courts of kings, but one royal lady, the Empress Frederick, was very gracious to me, and I am proud to remember her goodness. The Empress sent for me to tell her about some German excavations of Greek theatres, and to explain the new theory started by Dörpfeld as to the Greek stage. Hers was almost the saddest face I have ever seen, but she had the real sacred hunger for knowledge, and I am sure, had fate not broken her wings and caged her in a palace, she would have flown high. We were in the middle of eager talk when a servant came in and said the Prince of Wales (King Edward) wanted to see her. So little was I used to royal etiquette (which for the subject is simply the etiquette of servants) that I all but committed a *gaffe* by getting up to release her; —she saved me by shaking her head impatiently at the servant and saying "No, no," and turning to me, " Go on, go on, I must know." My future King had a good long wait. I saw the Empress again and again, and learnt to love her. But, oh how glad I was when I heard she was safely dead, dead and, though I could not know that then, spared the torture of the war. She bade me, when I next went to Greece, go and see her daughter, the Crown Princess of Greece. Of course I had to go, but I was sorry I went. The daughter was as common as the mother was distinguished. She had a bad Board-School accent and used slang. She did not really care about Greek things at all, but talked loudly about " our Waldstein who has made awfully jolly excavations ". She bored me as much as I bored her. Every one ought to see a little of royalties. It is so humbling and at first irritating to have to behave like a servant, and it makes you understand how servants really must feel.

Interviewers—after the first moment of excited importance—are not an interesting tribe, but one of them comes back to me with a whiff of fragrance, an American lady from the Middle West. A little old lady she was, with white curls and a Quaker bonnet, and romance in her heart. She brought a letter

of introduction and asked if I would visit her
in her Bloomsbury lodgings. I found her
there at eleven in the morning with a dainty
tea-tray before her; she must have spread it
with her own hands; no Bloomsbury landlady
was capable of it. She had heard, she said,
that we English ladies liked to drink a cup of
tea at eleven. She must have heard it below
stairs. And then began the interview. She
had been told that I was a great authority on
Greek vases, would I give her my idea on
"their place in modern education". I
began to stumble out a few platitudes. She
interrupted me with, "You'll excuse me,
Miss Harrison, but you're dropping pearls and
diamonds from your mouth, and I must get
out my pencil and notebook." Then, then
at last, out came the romance; she herself was
a "school teacher"; she had saved up her
money to come to Europe, not to see Europe
but to—write a book on Greek Art! Of
Greek and Greek Art she knew nothing, but,
pencil in hand, she was travelling round to the
museums of Europe to learn, and then, O
joy! to write: the gallantry and the innocence
of it! I don't know if that strangely com-
pounded book ever saw the light. It may be
death found her before she reached her Happy
Isles, but she had the spirit of Ulysses. Before
she left she asked, " Did I know Mr. Andrew

Lang?" She had a letter to him. "But", she said sadly, "my mind misgives me, Miss Harrison, that Mr. Andrew Lang is not an earnest seeker after truth."

And that reminds me of my first meeting with "Andrew of the brindled hair", at a dinner-party. Our hostess brought him up to me and, with a misguided desire to be pleasant, said, "You know Miss Harrison, and I am sure you have read her delightful books." "Don't know Miss Harrison," muttered Andrew, "never read her delightful books, don't want to," etc. (Oh, Andrew, and you had reviewed those "delightful books" not too delightedly!) "Come, Mr. Lang," I said, "we're both hungry, and I promise not to say a single word to you. Be a man." Alas! I broke my word. It was an enchanting dinner.

CHAPTER III

GREECE AND RUSSIA

ALL through my London life (fifteen years)
I lectured there and in the provinces. Being
one of a family of twelve, my fortune was
slender, and social life is costly. I regret
those lecturing years. I was voluble and had
instant success, but it was mentally demoralis-
ing and very exhausting. Though I was
almost fatally fluent, I could never face a big
audience without a sinking in the pit of what
is now called the *solar plexus*. Moreover, I
was lecturing on art, a subject for which I had
no natural gifts. My reactions to art are,
I think, always second-hand; hence, about
art, I am docile and open to persuasion. In
literature I am absolutely sure of my own
tastes, and a whole Bench of Bishops could
not alter my convictions. Happily, however,
bit by bit, art and archæology led to mythology,
mythology merged in religion; there I was at
home. All through my London life I
worked very hard—but, no! I remember

63

that Professor Gilbert Murray once told me
that I had never done an hour's really hard
work in my life. I think he forgets that I
have learnt the Russian declensions, which
is more than he ever did. But I believe he is
right. He mostly is. I never work in the
sense of attacking a subject against the grain,
tooth and nail. The kingdom of heaven
from me " suffereth no violence ". The
Russian verb " to learn " takes the dative,
which seems odd till you find out that it is
from the same root as " to get used to ".
When you learn you " get yourself used to "
a thing. That is worth a whole treatise of
pedagogy. And it explained to me my own
processes. One reads round a subject, soaks
oneself in it, and then one's personal responsi-
bility is over; something stirs and ferments,
swims up into your consciousness, and you
know you have to write a book. That may
not be " hard work ", but let me tell Professor
Murray it is painfully and pleasantly like it in
its results; it leaves you spent, washed out, a
rag, but an exultant rag.

My London life was happily broken by
much going abroad. All my archæology was
taught me by Germans. The great Ernst
Curtius, of Olympian fame, took me round
the museums of Berlin. Heinrich Brunn

64

came to see me in my lodgings at Munich, where I was thriftily living on four marks a day. I remember his first visit—a knock, a huge figure looming in the doorway, a benevolent, bearded, spectacled face, and he presented himself with the words, " Brunn bin Ich ". Dörpfeld was my most honoured master—we always called him " Avtos ". He let me go with him on his *Peloponnesos Reise* and his *Insel Reise.* They were marvels of organisation, and the man himself was a miracle. He would hold us spellbound for a six hours' peripatetic lecture, only broken by an interval of ten minutes to partake of a goat's-flesh sandwich and *etwas frisches Bier.* Once I saw, to my sorrow, three Englishmen tailing away after the *frisches Bier.* I was more grieved than surprised. They were Oxford men—the (then) Provost of Oriel, the Principal of Brasenose and an eminent fellow of Balliol. It was worth many hardships to see forty German professors try to mount forty recalcitrant mules. My own horsemanship, as already hinted, is nothing to " write home about ", but compared to those German professors I am a centaur. How it all comes back to me, for only last month, to my great joy, I met the grandson of Ernst Curtius, Professor Robert Ernst Curtius, a worthy descendant.

Greece in those days held many adventures. To one of these I still look back with poignant shame for my own bad manners. We arrived at Vurkano, just as the monastery gates were closing, and were hospitably received. The Hegoumenos led me into supper, placed me by his side, and fed me with titbits from his own plate. The Greek clergy, even the monks who may not marry, are quite simple and friendly to women. After the Roman attitude, it is refreshing to be accepted as a man and a brother—if a weaker one—and not looked at with sour eyes as an incarnate snare. I remember at Tinos I was watching the procession of the miraculous Eikon; the priest carrying the Eikon saw that I was the only West-European woman struggling in a throng of men, and sent a young priest to fetch me to walk by his side. There I could safely watch all that went on, the bowings, the kissings of the Eikon, and the priests' splendid vestments, the cures. But to return to my Hegoumenos. After supper he said he had a question to ask me. He had heard that rich Englishmen had in their mouths " stranger " (or " guest ") teeth made of gold, and which moved. Was it true? It was. Had I in my mouth by any chance a stranger tooth? I had, I owned, one, but in the best Oriental fashion I deprecated any mention

66

of it. It was but a poor thing, made not of gold, but of an elephant's tusk. Did I ever take it out? Yes. When? "Oh," nervously, "only very early in the morning." After a short sleep—sleep in a Greek monastery is rarely for long—I woke. The Hegoumenos was seated at my bed-head telling his beads and . . . watching. Oh, why, why did I not take out that "stranger" tooth? I might so easily have made a good man happy. The Graiæ themselves pointed the way. But I was young, and youth is vain and cruel. He was too polite to press the matter, and withdrew himself, slowly and sadly. In about ten minutes he was back, his face dark with anger. A terrible scandal had arisen in the monastery, its sanctity was outraged; we must leave at once. For one bad moment I feared that the scandal was my wholly unchaperoned state. No such thing. With a Greek *the* great impropriety for a woman is to travel alone and unprotected. What had happened was this. The friend with whom I was travelling, after a feverish night spent in wrestling with the hosts of Midian, had gone out to get cool, seen a pump in the monastery courtyard, and incontinently proceeded to have a much-needed shower-bath. The news flew like wildfire through the Brotherhood, and the Hegou-

menos was summoned to purge the outrage.
I ruthlessly sacrificed my kind protector. The
" Lord ", I said, was young and ignorant; he
knew no Greek letters (a gross libel); he had
been born and reared not in Christian England,
but in a strange barbarian hyperborean land,
where raiment was scanty and Christian
modesty unknown. Would His Reverence
pardon the young man and teach him better?
Fired with missionary zeal, the Hegoumenos
sent for the " Lord ", and finding him dumb,
pointed to a place about an inch above his
wrists, told him that thus far, without danger
to his soul, could a Christian man wash himself. The " Lord " was heard to mutter to
himself words to the effect that he would
"jolly well like to put the Hegoumenos
under his own pump ". This I hastily trans-
lated into a solemn promise that while life
lasted the " Lord ", by the heads of his
fathers, would never exceed the limit. The
crisis passed. When we left next morning
we gave more than the wonted largesse in
the hope of atoning for the bath. But the
outraged saint was far too fine a Christian
and a gentleman to be won by money. The
adieus were frigid. We left under a cloud.
At parting I gave him my photograph. He
placed it below the Eikon of the Virgin and
solemnly commended me to her protection

against the spiritual dangers to which I was so obviously exposed.

Long after, I visited Mount Athos. Of course, as a woman I could not set foot on the sacred promontory. My friends started off elate in the early morning, to visit the monasteries. Mr. Logan Pearsall Smith, I remember, proudly led the way. We mere women were left behind on the yacht disconsolate. They came back in the evening after the usual Pauline adventures in baskets, and with them came some Mount Athos monks to see the ship and the women, and sell rosaries, etc. One of the monks—a Russian, I think, for I could not understand his Greek, gave me a sheet of letter-paper with, for heading, a brightly coloured picture of the Mountain Mother issuing from Mount Athos. He pointed to the picture and then to me, and then to the mountain, as though he would say: Well, we've smuggled in one woman anyhow. It was wonderful to find the Great Mother here in her own Thrace, and worshipped still not by women but by her own celibate priests, the Kouretes.

The British Legation, at Athens, kept open house, and in those days the cheery young men who dwelt there made it a pleasant place. It was the proud boast of some of them that they had never been up to the

Acropolis, and that they only knew one word of modern Greek and that was *sitheróthromos*, the Greek for railway station, by means of which they hoped shortly to make their escape. They pretended, of course, that they were frightened to death of me because of my Greek, and that they dare not ask me to dance. They maligned themselves; they feared nothing in the world except that they might have to apply their minds to something sometime. They might have said with Punch's malingering marine, "Well sir, it's this way with me. I eats well and I sleeps well, but when I sees a bit o' work, I's all of a tremble."

At Athens I met Samuel Butler. We were in the same hotel; he saw me dining alone and kindly crossed over to ask if he might join me. Of course I was delighted and looked forward to pleasant talks, but, alas! he wanted me only as a safety-valve for his theory on the woman-authorship of the Odyssey, and the buzzing of that crazy bee drowned all rational conversation.

The first time I went to Athens I had the luck to make a small archæological discovery. I was turning over the fragments in the Acropolis Museum, then little more than a lumber-room. In a rubbish pile in the corner, to my great happiness, I lighted on the small stone figure of a bear. The furry hind paw was sticking out and caught my eye. I immediately had her—it was manifestly a she-bear—brought out and honourably placed. She must have been set up originally in the precinct of Artemis Brauronia. Within this precinct, year by year, went on the *arkteia* or bear-service. No well-born Athenian would marry a girl unless she had accomplished her *bear-service*, unless she was, in a word, *confirmed* to Artemis. In the *Lysistrata* of Aristophanes the chorus of women chant of the benefits they have received from the state, and the sacred acts they had accomplished before they came to maturity, and say, " I, wearing a saffron robe, was a bear at the Brauronian festival." Always these well-born, well-bred little Athenian girls must, to the end of their days, have thought reverently of the Great She-Bear. Among the Apaches to-day, we are told, only ill-bred Americans or Europeans who have never had any " raising " would think of speaking of the Bear without his reverential prefix of " Ostin ", meaning " Old One ", the equivalent of the Roman senator.

Crete I visited again and again, and to Crete I owe the impulse to my two most serious books, the *Prolegomena to the Study of Greek Religion* and *Themis*. Somewhere about the turn of the century there had come to light in the palace of Cnossos a clay sealing which was a veritable little manual of primitive Cretan faith and ritual. I shall never forget the moment when Mr. Arthur Evans first showed it me. It seemed too good to be true. It represented the Great Mother standing on her own mountain with her attendant lions, and before her a worshipper in ecstasy. At her side, a shrine with "horns of consecration". And another sealing read the riddle of the horns. The Minotaur is seated on the royal throne, and the Minotaur is none other than the human King—God wearing the mask of a bull. Here was this ancient ritual of the Mother and the Son which long preceded the worship of the Olympians: here were the true *Prolegomena*. Then when, some years later, I again visited Crete, I met with the sequel that gave me the impulse to *Themis*, the *Hymn of the Kouretes* found in the temple of Diktaean Zeus. Here we have embodied the magical rite of the Mother and the Son, the induction of the Year-Spirit who long preceded the worship of the Father. My third book on Greek religion, the *Epilegomena*, is, in the main, a résumé of the two first, and an attempt to relate them to our modern religious outlook. I should like to apologise here for the clumsy and pedantic titles *Prolegomena* and *Epilegomena*, but they really express the relation of the two books to my central work— *Themis*.

Copenhagen possesses a small but valuable collection of vases, and I had long planned to go there. I was delighted when a friend offered to take me in his yacht. My childhood having been passed between sea and moor, I have always had a passion for the sea and for sailing; but I am a wretched sailor, and the friends who are kind enough to take me on their yachts have always cause for repentance. The voyage began with disaster. In the North Sea we met bad weather, and the vessel, a yawl of only 20 tons, was in some danger. When she got back to dock at Cowes, they told us it was a wonder we had not all gone to the bottom. The last thing I remember was crawling on deck and seeing above me waves mountain high that seemed as if they must fall and swallow us. Then I suppose I lost consciousness, for I woke—as I thought—in heaven, in utter bliss. Round me were kneeling angels in blue gowns and white caps with streamers. Under stress of weather we had put in at Heligoland, and they had landed me in a boat and, every hand being needed aboard, had left me lying on the shore, and the women of Heligoland crowded to see me. I suppose it was the relief from the heaving sea, but I knew then the extreme of physical rapture after physical anguish. We were weather-bound for a couple of days and then made our way into the Eider Canal, where all was peace. Arguing on philosophy all day long, for my host was a hard thinker as well as a bold and skilful seaman, we drifted through long lines of one-legged storks and into the Baltic, with its fiords and its beech trees, with their branches dipping into the water. The Baltic is a "short" unpleasant sea, but I remember with pride that I recovered sufficiently to steer the yacht into Copenhagen. There I learnt what honesty is. The keeper of the Museum met me the first day, but the second he was engaged. He left me a huge bunch of keys and the freedom of the place. I had the yacht's boat in the canal at the Museum door and could easily have looted the whole place. But it seems, among the hardy Norsemen, these things simply are not done. Yet in my own England, at the British Museum, when I am at work a member of the staff never leaves me. Ostensibly he is there to help me, but really as policeman. I remember Sir Francis Darwin telling me that in Stock-

JANE HARRISON AND HOPE MIRRLEES.

To face page 90.

holm he and a Swedish friend were crossing a bridge and they saw a gold watch lying on the pavement. Sir Francis stooped to pick it up and said: " I suppose we must take it to the police." " Oh no," said the Swede, " just put it on the parapet, where it will be safe; the man who lost it is sure to come back." I fancy if you left a gold watch on the parapet of London Bridge it would not wait long for its owner; yet we English are supposed to be an honest people.

Stockholm, whither I went to see the great prehistoric museum, was a sad disappointment. I had heard it called the " Venice of the North ". It is common to the verge of squalor. It contains one beautiful building, the architect of which was a Frenchman. I have come to realise that many people, if they see water and some islands or a lake, feel that it must be beautiful. In the same way they find mountains always beautiful and inspiring. The Matterhorn is, to me, one of the ugliest objects in all nature, like nothing on earth but a colossal extracted fang turned upside down, but all the same, every night during the season, the terrace of the Riffel Alp's Hotel is crowded with archdeacons gazing raptly at the Matterhorn and praising God for the beauties of His handiwork.

To Petersburg I journeyed solely and
simply to study the Kertsch antiquities in the
Hermitage. I knew no word of Russian, and
cared nothing then for Russia; my eyes were
blinded for the moment by the "glory that
was Greece". I had taken letters from the
British Museum, and was at once shown into
a gorgeous room in which sat a still more
gorgeous official, smoking cigarettes. He
was all courtesy and kindness—what could
he do for me? Did I know So-and-so? Had
I seen this and that?—but no mention of
Kertsch. I am now convinced that, though
he must have known the name, he had no
notion of its archæological significance, nor
even that it had been an Athenian colony.
At last, timidly, I tried to state my business.
Could I have the vases out of their cases, and
was there yet any material unpublished by
Stephani that I could have access to? He
looked rather blank, and then with a sort of
twinkle in his deep-set eyes said if there was
anything about social matters or the court in
which he could help me, would I command
him; but as for these learned matters, would I
pardon him if he referred me to the gentleman
who was good enough to act as his brains.
Here he significantly touched his handsome
empty head. He took me to a distant room
where a shabby German Pole was at work,

surrounded by papers and potsherds. He proved an efficient specialist. I saw my noble backwoodsman no more—no doubt he was gladly rid of the " mad Englishwoman ". I couldn't help liking the friendly creature; he had the simple, perfect manners of which Russians hold the secret. But in those days I was a ferocious moralist, and his quite open and shameless inadequacy made a premature Bolshevist of me. But oh, what a fool, what an idiot I was to leave Russia without knowing it! I might so easily have made the pilgrimage to Tolstoy; I might even have seen Dostoevsky. It has been all my life my besetting sin that I could only see one thing at a time. I was blinded by over-focus. I am bitterly, eternally punished. Never now shall I see Moscow and Kiev, cities of my dreams.

Literally of my dreams. Twice only in my life have I dreamt a significant dream. This is one. One night soon after the Russian revolution I dreamt I was in a great, ancient forest—what in Russian would be called " a dreaming wood ". In it was cleared a round space, and the space was crowded with huge bears softly dancing. I somehow knew that I had come to teach them to dance the Grand Chain in the Lancers, a square dance now obsolete. I was not the least afraid, only very glad and proud. I went up and began trying to make them join hands and form a circle. It was no good. I tried and tried, but they only shuffled away, courteously waving their paws, intent on their own mysterious doings. Suddenly I knew that these doings were more wonderful and beautiful than any Grand Chain (as, indeed, they might well be!). It was for me to learn, not to teach. I woke up crying, in an ecstasy of humility.

That may stand for what Russia has meant to me. And let there be no misunderstanding. It is not "the Slav soul" that drew me. Not even, indeed, Russian literature. Of course, years before I had read and admired Turgenev and Tolstoy and Dostoevsky, but at least by the two last I was more frightened than allured. I half resented their probing poignancy, and some passages, like the end of the *Idiot* and the scene between Dimitri Karamasov and Grushenka, seemed to me in their poignancy to pass the limits of the permissible in art. They hurt too badly and too inwardly. No, it was not these portentous things that laid a spell upon me. It was just the Russian language. If I could have my life over again, I would devote it not to art or literature, but to language. Life itself may hit one hard, but always, always one can take sanctuary in language. Language is as much an art and as sure a refuge as painting or music or literature. It reflects and interprets and makes bearable life; only it is a wider, because more subconscious, life.

CONCLUSION

I HAVE spoken much of people, nothing of books—yet the influence of books on my life has been intimate and incessant. When I first came to London I became a Life Member of the London Library. London life was costly, but I felt that, if the worst came to the worst, with a constant supply of books and a small dole for tobacco, I could cheerfully face the Workhouse. Three books stand out as making three stages in my thinking : Aristotle's *Ethics*, Bergson's *L'Évolution créatrice* and Freud's *Totemism and Taboo*. By nature I was a Platonist, but Aristotle, I think, helped me more than Plato. It happened that the *Ethics* was among the set books for my year at Cambridge. To realise the release that Aristotle brought, you must have been reared as I was in a narrow school of Evangelicalism—reared with sin always present, with death and judgement before you, Hell and Heaven to either hand. It was like coming out of a madhouse into a quiet college quadrangle where all was liberty and sanity, and you became a law to yourself. The doctrine of virtue as the Mean—what an uplift and revelation to one "born in sin"! The notion of the *summum bonum* as an " energy ", as an exercise of personal faculty, to one who had been taught that God claimed all, and the notion of the "perfect life" that was to include as a matter of course friendship. I remember walking up and down in the College garden, thinking could it possibly be true, were the chains really broken and the prison doors open.

In 1907 came *L'Évolution créatrice.* Off and on I had read philosophy all my life, from Heracleitos to William James, but of late years I had read it less and less, feeling that I got nothing new, only a ceaseless shuffling of the cards, a juggling with the same glass balls, and then suddenly it seemed this new Moses struck the rock and streams gushed forth in the desert. But I need not tell of an experience shared in those happy years by every thinking man in Europe.

With Freud it was quite different. By temperament I am, if not a prude, at least a Puritan, and at first the ugliness of it all sickened me. I hate a sick-room, and have a physical fear of all obsessions and insanity. Still I struggled on, feeling somehow that behind and below all this sexual mud was something big and real. Then fortunately I lighted on *Totemism and Taboo*, and at once the light broke and I felt again the sense of release. Here was a big constructive imagination; here was a mere doctor laying bare the origins of Greek drama as no classical scholar had ever done, teaching the anthropologist what was really meant by his *totem and taboo*, probing the mysteries of sin, of sanctity, of sacrament—a man who, because he understood, purged the human spirit from fear. I have no confidence in psycho-analysis as a method of therapeutics. I am sure that Mr. Roger-Fry is right and Freud quite wrong as to the psychology of art, but I am equally sure that for generations almost every branch of human knowledge will be enriched and illumined by the imagination of Freud.

Looking back over my own life, I see with what halting and stumbling steps I made my way to my own special subject. Greek literature as a specialism I early felt was barred to me. The only field of research that the Cambridge of my day knew of was textual criticism, and for fruitful work in that my scholarship was never adequate. We Hellenists were, in truth, at that time a " people who sat in darkness ", but we were

soon to see a great light, two great lights
—archæology, anthropology. Classics were
turning in their long sleep. Old men began
to see visions, young men to dream dreams.
I had just left Cambridge when Schliemann
began to dig at Troy. Among my own
contemporaries was J. G. Frazer, who was
soon to light the dark wood of savage supersti-
tion with a gleam from *The Golden Bough*.
The happy title of that book—Sir James
Frazer has a veritable genius for titles—made
it arrest the attention of scholars. They saw
in comparative anthropology a serious subject
actually capable of elucidating a Greek or
Latin text. Tylor had written and spoken;
Robertson Smith, exiled for heresy, had seen
the Star in the East; in vain; we classical
deaf-adders stopped our ears and closed our
eyes; but at the mere sound of the magical
words " Golden Bough " the scales fell—
we heard and understood. Then Arthur
Evans set sail for his new Atlantis and tele-
graphed news of the Minotaur from his own
labyrinth; perforce we saw this was a serious
matter, it affected the " Homeric Question ".

By nature, I am sure, I am not an archæo-
logist — still less an anthropologist — the
" beastly devices of the heathen " weary and
disgust me. But, borne along by the irresistible tide of adventure, I dabbled in both

archæology and anthropology, and I am glad
I did, for both were needful for my real
subject—religion. When I say " religion ",
I am instantly obliged to correct myself; it
is not religion, it is ritual that absorbs me. I
have elsewhere[1] tried to show that Art is not
the handmaid of Religion, but that Art in
some sense springs out of Religion, and that
between them is a connecting link, a bridge,
and that bridge is Ritual. On that bridge,
emotionally, I halt. It satisfies something
within me that is appeased by neither Religion
nor Art. A ritual dance, a ritual procession
with vestments and lights and banners, move
me as no sermon, no hymn, no picture, no
poem has ever moved me; perhaps it is because
a procession seems to me like life, like *durée*
itself, caught and fixed before me. Only
twice have I seen a ritual dance, and first
the dance of the Seises before the high altar
in the Cathedral at Seville. It was at Carnival
time I saw it. I felt instantly that it was
frankly Pagan. Its origin is, as the Roman
Church frankly owns, " perdue dans la nuit
des temps "—we can but conjecture that it
took its rise in the dances of the Kouretes
of Crete to Mother and Son. The dance
was accompanied by a prayer to the setting
sun, a prayer for light and healing. The

[1] *Art and Ritual* (Home University Library).

movements executed by six choristers are attenuated to a single formal step. It is decorous, even prim, like some stiff stylised shadow. But it is strangely moving in the fading light with the wondrous setting of the high altar and the golden grille, and above all the sound of the harsh, plangent Spanish voices. Great Pan, indeed, is dead—his ghost still dances.

Only last year I saw a wondrous ritual procession, a marked contrast to the Seville dance. It is held at Echternach each year, on the Tuesday after Pentecost. It is, I think, the most living survival of the ritual dance to be seen in Europe. Thanks to the kindness of a Luxembourgoise lady, Madame Emil Mayerisch de Saint Hubert, I was able to observe it in every detail. The dancing procession is held now in honour of our Saxon saint, St. Willibrord, but obviously it goes back to magical days. The dancers muster at the bridge below the little town and, gathering numbers as they go, dance through the streets, halting here and there and ending in the Basilica. As the dance is magical, it is essential that the whole town should be traversed. The clergy are in attendance, any one and every one dances or rather leaps, for it is a jumping step; like the Cretan Kouretes they " leap for health and wealth ".

I saw an old, old woman, scarcely able to walk, but she " lifted her foot in the dance ". I saw a woman with a sick baby in her arms, and she danced for healing; but most of all it was the young men, the Kouretes, who danced.

The ritual dance is all but dead, but the ritual drama, the death and the resurrection of the Year-Spirit, still goes on. I realised this when I first heard Mass celebrated according to the Russian, that is substantially the Greek rite. There you have the real enacting of a mystery—the mystery of the death and resurrection of the Year-Spirit which preceded drama. It is hidden, out of sight; the priest comes out from behind the golden gate to announce the accomplishment. It is the coming out of the Messenger in a Greek play to announce the Death and the Resurrection. The Roman Church has sadly marred its mystery. The rite of consecration is performed in public before the altar and loses thereby half its significance.

I mention these ritual dances, this ritual drama, this bridge between art and life, because it is things like these that I was all my life blindly seeking. A thing has little charm for me unless it has on it the patina of age. Great things in literature, Greek plays for example, I most enjoy when behind their bright splendours I see moving darker and older shapes. That must be my *apologia pro vita mea.*

At the close of one's reminiscences it is fitting that one should say something as to how life looks at the approach of Death. As to Death, when I was young, personal immortality seemed to me axiomatic. The mere thought of Death made me furious. I was so intensely alive I felt I could defy any one, anything—God, or demon, or Fate herself— to put me out. All that is changed now. If I think of Death at all it is merely as a negation of life, a close, a last and necessary chord. What I dread is disease, that is, bad, disordered life, not Death, and disease, so far, I have escaped. I have no hope whatever of personal immortality, no desire even for a future life. My consciousness began in a very humble fashion with my body; with my body, very quietly, I hope it will end.

Nox est perpetua una dormienda.

And then there is another thought. We are told now that we bear within us the seeds, not of one, but of two lives—the life of the race and the life of the individual. The life of the race makes for racial immortality; the life of the individual suffers *l'attirance de la mort*, the lure of death; and this from the outset. The unicellular animals are practically immortal; the complexity of the individual spells death. The unmarried and the childless cut themselves loose from racial immortality, and are dedicate to individual life—a side track, a blind alley, yet surely a supreme end in itself. By what miracle I escaped marriage I do not know, for all my life long I fell in love. But, on the whole, I am glad. I do not doubt that I lost much, but I am quite sure I gained more. Marriage, for a woman at least, hampers the two things that made life to me glorious—friendship and learning. In man it was always the friend, not the husband, that I wanted. Family life has never attracted me. At its best it seems to me rather narrow and selfish; at its worst, a private hell. The rôle of wife and mother is no easy one; with my head full of other things I might have dismally failed. On the other hand, I have a natural gift for community life. It seems to me sane and civilised and economically right. I like to live spaciously, but rather plainly, in large halls with great spaces and quiet libraries. I like to wake in the morning with the sense of a great, silent garden round me. These things are, or should be, and soon will be, forbidden to the private family; they are right and good for the community. If I had been rich I should have founded a learned community for women, with vows of consecration and a beautiful rule and habit; as it is, I am content to have lived many years of my life in a college. I think, as civilisation advances, family life will become, if not extinct, at least much modified and curtailed.

Old age, believe me, is a good and pleasant thing. It is true you are gently shouldered off the stage, but then you are given such a comfortable front stall as spectator, and, if you have really played your part, you are more than content to sit down and watch. All life has become a thing less strenuous, softer and warmer. You are allowed all sorts of comfortable little physical licences; you may doze through dull lectures, you may go to bed early when you are bored. The young all pay you a sort of tender deference to which you know you have no real claim. Every one is solicitous to help you; it seems the whole world offers you a kind, protecting arm. Life does not cease when you are old, it only suffers a rich change. You go on loving, only your love, instead of a burning, fiery furnace, is the mellow glow of an autumn sun. You even go on falling in love, and for the same foolish reasons—the tone of a voice, the glint of a strangely set eye—only you fall so gently; and in old age you may even show a man that you like to be with him without his wanting to marry you or thinking you want to marry him.

But then " old age is lonely ". Not if you follow my example! My friends, men and women, are most of them some twenty years younger than I am. I have only one friend made in my 'seventies, Mr. Guy le Strange, if he will let me so account him. He taught me, with infinite patience and kindness, when I was over seventy the elements of Persian, a sure road to my heart. And, I admit, Fate has been very kind to me. In my old age she has sent me, to comfort me, a ghostly daughter, dearer than any child after the flesh, more gifted than any possible offspring of Aunt Glegg.

I should like to run on and tell of my life since I left Cambridge. For leave Cambridge, with measureless regret, I did. I began to feel that I had lived too long the strait Academic life with my mind intently focussed on the solution of a few problems. I wanted before the end came to see things more freely and more widely, and, above all, to get the new focus of another civilisation.

CONCLUSION

Russia, my "Land of Heart's Desire", was closed to me. France and America in France have received me with a kindness I can neither repay nor forget.

If only I might tell of the wonderful new friends, French and Russian, I have made in Paris and at Pontigny! But these things are too present, too intimate—so my tale must end.

AMERICAN WOMEN'S UNIVERSITY CLUB,
4 RUE DE CHEVREUSE, PARIS.

CPSIA information can be obtained
at www.ICGtesting.com
Printed in the USA
BVHW030919180822
644923BV00007B/179

9 781013 370755